HOW DOES IT WORK?: FARM TECH
GREENHOUSES

by Johannah Luza

Ideas for Parents and Teachers

Pogo Books let children practice reading informational text while introducing them to nonfiction features such as headings, labels, sidebars, maps, and diagrams, as well as a table of contents, glossary, and index.

Carefully leveled text with a strong photo match offers early fluent readers the support they need to succeed.

Before Reading

• "Walk" through the book and point out the various nonfiction features. Ask the student what purpose each feature serves.

• Look at the glossary together. Read and discuss the words.

Read the Book

• Have the child read the book independently.

• Invite him or her to list questions that arise from reading.

After Reading

• Discuss the child's questions. Talk about how he or she might find answers to those questions.

• Prompt the child to think more. Ask: What is one example of new greenhouse technology? How does it help people grow crops more efficiently?

Pogo Books are published by Jump!
5357 Penn Avenue South
Minneapolis, MN 55419
www.jumplibrary.com

Library of Congress Cataloging-in-Publication Data

Names: Luza, Johannah, author.
Title: Greenhouses / by Johannah Luza.
Description: Minneapolis, MN: Jump!, Inc., [2024]
Series: How does it work? Farm tech | Includes index.
Audience: Ages 7-10
Identifiers: LCCN 2023003997 (print)
LCCN 2023003998 (ebook)
ISBN 9798885246880 (hardcover)
ISBN 9798885246897 (paperback)
ISBN 9798885246903 (ebook)
Subjects: LCSH: Greenhouses–Juvenile literature.
Classification: LCC SB415 .L89 2024 (print)
LCC SB415 (ebook)
DDC 635.9/823–dc23/eng/20230215
LC record available at https://lccn.loc.gov/2023003997
LC ebook record available at https://lccn.loc.gov/2023003998

Editor: Eliza Leahy
Designer: Emma Almgren-Bersie
Content Consultant: Santosh K. Pitla, Ph.D., Biological Systems Engineering

Photo Credits: Daan Kloeg/Shutterstock, cover; darioayala/Shutterstock, 1; Geo-grafika/Shutterstock, 3; Okayanstvo/Shutterstock, 4; BearFotos/Shutterstock, 5; Adrian Eugen Ciobaniuc/Shutterstock, 6; Xinhua/Alamy, 6-7, 17, 18-19; Try_my_best/Shutterstock, 8-9; Robert Bodnar/iStock, 10; Shutterstock, 11; Satyrenko/Shutterstock, 12-13; Lano Lan/Shutterstock, 14-15; sunsetman/Shutterstock, 16; Richard Levine/Alamy, 20-21; fcafotodigital/iStock, 23.

Printed in the United States of America at Corporate Graphics in North Mankato, Minnesota.

TABLE OF CONTENTS

CHAPTER 1

WHAT IS A GREENHOUSE?

A greenhouse isn't green. So why is it called that? It is a building in which plants grow! No matter the weather, plants can grow year-round in a greenhouse.

This means fresh fruit and vegetables in winter. Farmers can sell more **crops** throughout the year. They can also grow plants that might not typically grow in their area.

Greenhouses protect plants. Insects and animals that eat them can't get in. When strawberries are grown outside, birds are often first to get them. If they are grown in a greenhouse, you get first pick!

Greenhouses also protect against weather. They provide shelter from snow, hail, and wind. They help protect against **drought** or too much rain. They keep the temperature just right. How? Let's find out!

DID YOU KNOW?

The first greenhouse was built almost 2,000 years ago! The **emperor** of Rome was ill. His doctor told him to eat one cucumber a day to get better. A greenhouse was built to grow them all year. It was made of stone and glass.

CHAPTER 2

HOW GREENHOUSES WORK

Greenhouse walls and roofs are made of **transparent** glass or plastic. Why? These materials let sunlight in. Plants need sunlight to grow.

They also need warm temperatures. The plants and greenhouse floor **absorb** sunlight. Sunlight turns to heat. Heat gets trapped. It warms the air.

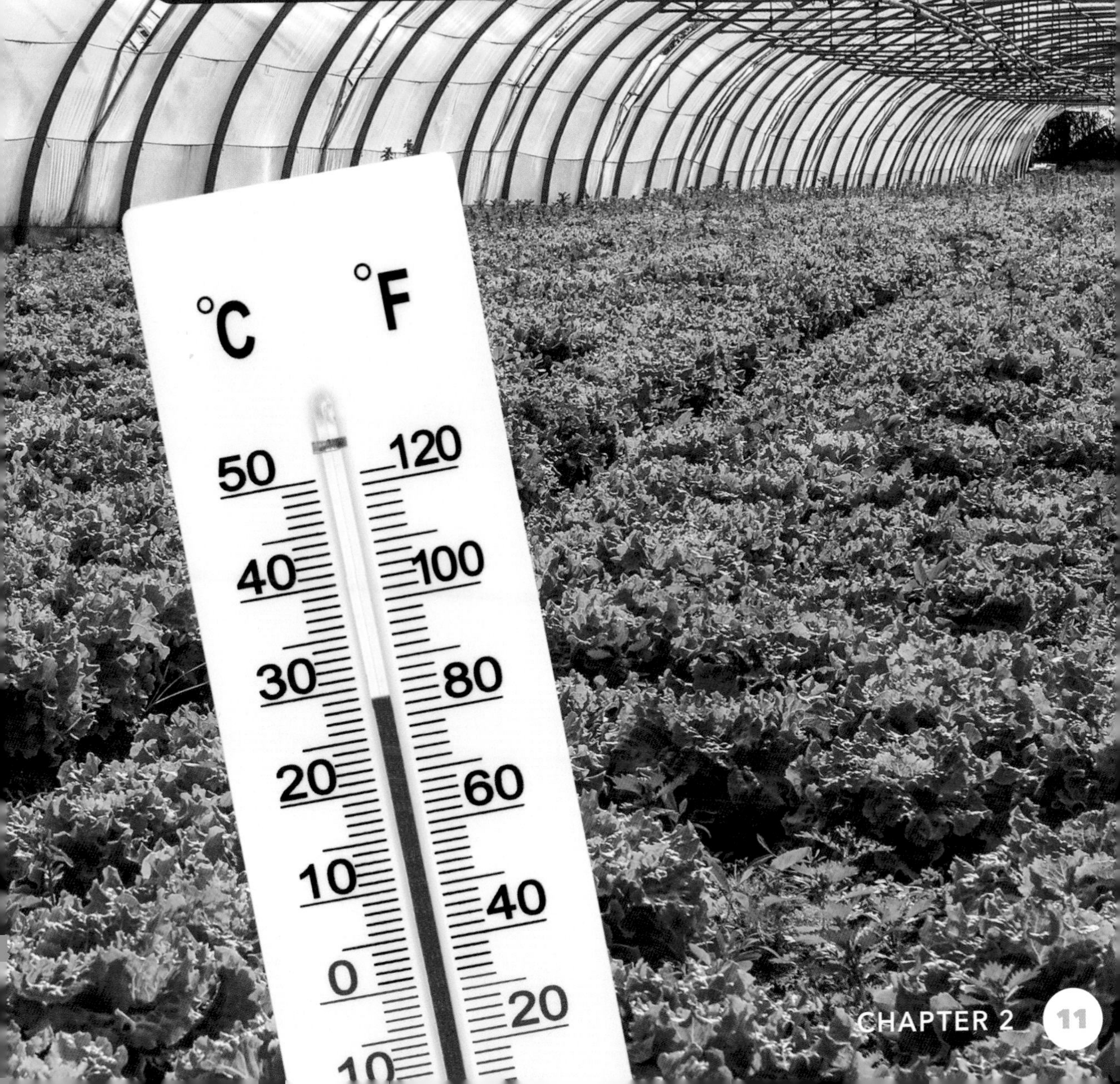

°C °F

50 120

40 100

30 80

20 60

10 40

0 20

sprayer

Plants are watered by hand or with timed sprayers. Fans and vents keep the temperature and **moisture** just right. They help water **evaporate**. If more moisture is needed, water is sprayed on the floors. Buckets of water are placed inside.

TAKE A LOOK!

How does a greenhouse help plants grow? Take a look!

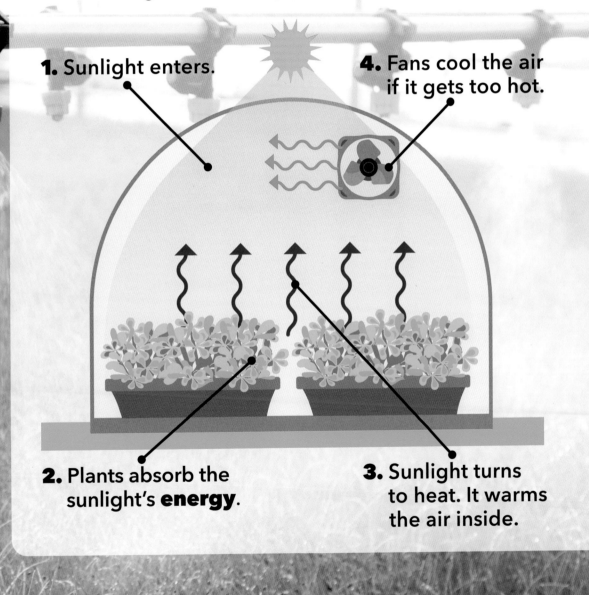

1. Sunlight enters.

4. Fans cool the air if it gets too hot.

2. Plants absorb the sunlight's **energy**.

3. Sunlight turns to heat. It warms the air inside.

Greenhouses can also be used for **hydroponics**. This **method** allows plants to grow in water. They don't need soil. **Nutrients** are added to the water. These feed the plants. A pump sends water to the plants many times a day. Timers control the flow of water.

TAKE A LOOK!

How does a hydroponic greenhouse work? Take a look!

3. Drip lines deliver water and nutrients to plants.

2. A pump pushes water and nutrients through tubes.

1. Water collects in a tank.

CHAPTER 3

NEW METHODS

Aeroponics is a new method of growing plants. It is similar to hydroponics. It doesn't use soil. But it uses less water.

roots

Aeroponics uses mist. Nutrients are added to water. It is sprayed onto plants' roots.

Many aeroponics systems save space, too. How? On most farms, crops are grown outside. They are planted in rows. This takes up a lot of space.

Vertical farming is often done in greenhouses. This method takes up 99 percent less land than farming in rows! This gives us more land and food.

With new farming technology and methods, greenhouses are feeding more people. How else can greenhouses help us?

DID YOU KNOW?

The world's largest rooftop greenhouse is in Canada. It feeds more than 10,000 families each year!

ACTIVITIES & TOOLS

MAKE A MINI GREENHOUSE

See how greenhouses help plants grow in this fun activity!

What You Need:
- pushpin
- two clear plastic cups
- potting soil
- three sunflower seeds
- spray bottle filled with water
- tape
- tray or plate

1 **Use the pushpin to poke several holes in the bottom of one cup. Ask an adult if you need help.**

2 **Fill the cup nearly to the top with potting soil. Pat it down gently.**

3 **Place three sunflower seeds in the soil. Leave some space between each seed.**

4 **Cover the seeds with a scoop of soil and pat down gently.**

5 **Use the spray bottle to water the seeds.**

6 **Place the other cup upside down on top of the cup with the seeds to make the greenhouse roof. Tape one side together like a hinge.**

7 **Put your greenhouse on a tray or plate. Place it near a window that will get plenty of sunlight.**

8 **Spray the soil with water every day. It won't be long before you see some sprouts!**

absorb: To soak up liquid.

aeroponics: A method of growing plants in which a plant's roots hang in the air and receive a mist filled with nutrients.

crops: Plants grown for food or profit.

drought: A long period without rain.

emperor: The male ruler of an empire.

energy: The ability of something to do work.

evaporate: To change into a vapor or gas.

hydroponics: A method of growing plants in which a plant's roots receive nutrients by being submerged in water.

method: A particular way of doing something.

moisture: Wetness from rain, snow, dew, or fog.

nutrients: Substances such as proteins, minerals, or vitamins that plants and animals need to stay healthy.

transparent: Clear and able to let light through.

vertical farming: The practice of growing plants on vertical surfaces, such as walls, instead of horizontally in rows.

INDEX

TO LEARN MORE

Finding more information is as easy as 1, 2, 3.

① **Go to www.factsurfer.com**

② **Enter "greenhouses" into the search box.**

③ **Choose your book to see a list of websites.**

FACT SURFER